Getting Off
on the
Right Foot

A Survival Guide
for New Teachers

Compiled by
Dave Puckett

Incentive Publications
Nashville, Tennessee

Education World, a web-based magazine for teachers, asked the "sophomores" who faced—and survived—that dreaded first year to reflect on their successes and failures. First-year teachers, here is their best advice for getting through it. The rest of this booklet is organized around this article rich with "sophomore advice" used by permission of *Education World.*

Illustrated by Kris Sexton
Cover by Geoffrey Brittingham
Edited by Jill Norris
Copy edited by Stephanie McGuirk

ISBN 978-0-86530-508-3

1   2   3   4   5   6   7   8   9   10   11   10   09   08

PRINTED IN THE UNITED STATES OF AMERICA
www.incentivepublications.com

Table of Contents

Message for Teachers
New to the Middle Level

Congratulations! It's official! You are now a Middle School Teacher! You aced your education courses, know your core content for assessment inside and out, can leap to the highest level of Bloom's taxonomy in a single bound, and finally have an actual job with an official class list. You may be brand new to teaching, brand new to the middle level, or entering the profession as a second career. You are bright. You are motivated. You are credentialed.

Only one problem remains. School starts soon, and you don't have a clue what to do first. As in most of life, a good place to begin is at the beginning. On the first day of school, the real secret to success is in the planning. This survival guide is designed to help you think about that planning.

It will also help you come to terms with the reality of the magnificent task you are undertaking. With its practical advice, encouraging asides, and humor, this guide will not bore you. As you browse the pages, jot down any ideas or "ahas!" and use these notes to guide your preparations.

Fran Salyers
Kentucky Middle School Association

Advice from the Sophomores

There's no doubt about it. Beginning the school year in a strange environment filled with new faces, unfamiliar procedures, and unknown pitfalls can be a scary prospect. You're the teacher, however, and you can "never let 'em see you sweat."

To help you stay cool and dry in the coming year, *Education World* asked the "sophomores" who faced—and survived—that dreaded first year to reflect on their successes and failures. What advice did those teachers offer?

From North Carolina to Arizona, from Mississippi to Wisconsin, the "grizzled veterans" agreed on several essential points:

Take charge.

Wisconsin teacher Dawn Schurman recommended "having a clear discipline plan set up, with both rewards and consequences. Explain it to the kids on day one and review throughout the first week." In addition, she reports, "I'm very glad that I sent home a copy of the discipline plan. I asked parents to read it with their child and to each sign and return a contract stating that they agreed to the rules. This has come in handy a few times."

First-year teacher Jean Federico said, "I have one big piece of advice for first-year teachers: before the first day of school, have plenty of activities prepared for emergency use. I learned the hard way that kids will misbehave if they have nothing to do. A class full of bored kids won't all sit quietly for ten minutes waiting for you to figure out what is next."

Keep students busy and engaged.

Get peer support.

Retta Threet, a teacher in Sumter, South Carolina, admitted, "My biggest mistake was not insisting on a mentor, or at least a peer teacher. If I had it to do again, I would make a good friend to whom I could go for advice."

Get parental support.

North Carolina teacher Jana Lippe suggested, "Use your parents as much as you can. Every time I needed supplies for a celebration, I just sent a note home asking for donations. Every time, the parents came through."

Arizona English teacher Alana Morales advised, "Find an organization system that you can live and work with and stick with it. With 120-plus students, it's crucial that you stay organized!"

Organize yourself.

Organize your students.

Mississippi teacher Lisa Packard suggests, "Don't assume they know how to organize themselves, because they don't. Show them how to organize their notebooks and folders. Show them exactly what you want on their papers and homework."

Teacher Mike Powell advised, "Start keeping a professional journal. After your first year, this journal will allow you to reflect on your professional practices and to witness what is probably going to be enormous personal growth."

Write and reflect.

Have fun!

"Do your best and have fun doing it. Once I finally relaxed, I had a great time," said teacher Tracy Keirns.

So, with thanks to Dawn, Jean, Retta, Jana, Alana, Lisa, Tracy, Lew, Mike, and all the other teachers who responded to our request, *Education World* compiled a list of the 26 top tips for surviving the first year. See "The ABC's for First-Year Teachers" on the next page.

from *www.education-world.com*

The ABC's for First-Year Teachers

Admit your mistakes—and learn from them.

Be firm but flexible.

Communicate with parents.

Develop a homework policy—and stick to it.

Empower your students; don't just lecture to them.

Find time to attend after-school events.

Get to know all the teachers in your school and make friends
with the cooks, custodians, aides, and secretaries.

Have the courage to try something else
if what you're doing isn't working.

Institute a clear discipline policy—and enforce it consistently.

Just listen—both to what the kids are saying
and to what they're not saying.

Keep a journal.

Learn your school's policies and procedures.

Model desired attitudes and behavior.

Non carborundum ignorami.
(Don't let the imbeciles wear you down.)

Overplan.

Prepare interesting lessons.

Quit worrying and just do your best.

Remember that you teach students first,
then you teach whatever academic discipline you learned.

Stay alert.

Take pictures.

Understand that the learning process involves
everyone—teachers, students, colleagues, and parents—
and get everyone involved.

Volunteer to share projects and ideas, and don't be afraid
to ask others to share their ideas with you.

Work within your limits.

e**X**pect the unexpected—and plan for it!

Yell if you need support.

Zero in on your strengths, not your weaknesses.
(Remember—nobody's perfect!)

PART 1

Prepare to Begin . . . Before You Begin!

Prepare Yourself

Many teachers fill their classrooms with collections of their favorite things. Coffee mugs, ceramic apples, even plush animals decorate middle school classrooms across the land. But, there are a few personal items that should be prominent in every teacher's classroom regardless of experience or expertise. Let's call these the "Big Four."

 ## The Teacher's Reflective Journal

Take a few minutes at the end of each day to make notes on your thoughts and impressions about the day's events. Did your lesson go really well, or really badly? Why? Did a difficult discipline problem arise? How did you handle it? What was the result? How would you do it differently next time? What successes did you experience? What compliments did you receive?

As the year goes on, your journal will help you identify what works and what doesn't, and it will help you think about alternatives. The journal will document your growth as a teacher. So often we make the mistake of not taking time to recognize our own growth. Protect your journaling time jealously; there may eventually even be a book in it!

 ## The Personal Appointment Calendar

One of the greatest assistants you will ever possess is known by several names . . . your personal planner, appointment book, PDA, or agenda. Regardless of what you call it, use it! A personal planner will help you with reminders of faculty meetings, professional development sessions, and scheduled observations. But more importantly, it can be used to document the unscheduled events which invariably crop up during the day, and often come back to haunt you later if you forget. You may think you will remember that Shawn's father asked for a list of suggested sources for extra credit work, or what you need to have with you for the next department meeting, but why take chances?

Keep your planner where you will always have access to it. Since much of what you enter in the way of notes may be personal in nature, it is a good idea to keep your planner in your desk, not on it!

 ## #3 A Personal Survival Kit

Somewhere out of the reach of students, arrange to store a personal survival kit. In it you may wish to include those little things you don't normally need, but when you need them, you really need them! Include such items as:

- a small sewing kit
- safety pins
- Band-Aids
- antacids
- cough drops
- change
- snacks (instant soup, instant hot chocolate, fat-free pretzels, plastic silverware, etc.)
- breath mints
- tissues
- hand lotion (paperwork really dries you out!)
- a spare pair of socks (which do match) or pantyhose, as the case may be
- basic "fix-it-quick" tools (small screwdriver and extra screws for eyeglass repairs)
- any other items which may make a bad day or a minor catastrophe a little easier to deal with. None of these has any bearing on your success as a teacher, but having them handy will make life a lot less stressful.

 ## #4 A Big Canvas Tote Bag To Keep It All In!

Prepare the Way

You will feel a lot more confident the first day of school if you have invested some time in becoming familiar with your surroundings and the people with whom you will be working. Before school officially opens, you may wish to:

- **Familiarize yourself with the school buildings and grounds.** You really weren't able to absorb much during the five minute tour the principal gave you after your interview. Take time to explore, observe, and become comfortable with key locations. Locate the bathrooms (not just the one closest to your classroom), the gym, cafeteria, the media center, the teacher's lounge. Find out where audio-visual equipment is stored, and how to check it out.

- **Visit the school Web site.** A school Web site can provide valuable information about the school and its community, as well as insight into what is expected of teachers and students. Find out how to get your e-mail address.

- **Review the school's policies and procedures.** Ask about any procedures that are unclear or are not covered in the teacher's handbook. Learn the reason behind policies which may not make sense. Every school has its history and problems. You will be better equipped to follow policies and procedures correctly if you understand the reasoning behind them.

- **Make friends with the most important school support staff.** The best friends a teacher can have are the school secretary, the cafeteria manager, and the head custodian. Introduce yourself. Remember names. Make it clear that you expect to make mistakes at first and that you realize that they might be inconvenienced. Ask how you can make their lives easier. Bring doughnuts!

- **Make a friend.** Choose a teacher at your grade level or within your content department, or simply in a nearby classroom, and ask if he or she would be available to answer questions or give friendly advice during the first few weeks of school. Ask a lot of questions. And don't apologize for asking. You need to know, so asking is what you should do. Your new friend will want to help and will know the best way to provide help, so your questions are important.

Don't assume very much. Ask for clarification or check it out. You have a lot to learn, especially in the first two or three years, so don't feel inadequate or embarrassed asking often for suggestions or advice. Let your new friend know that you are open to suggestions and eager to learn. Look to veteran teachers to share lesson plans which put core content into practice. Expect them to offer tips on practical problems you didn't learn about in school. Ask veteran teachers to allow you to observe their classrooms and invite them to observe yours. Seek the help of a mentor who has the skills and knowledge you would like to develop. Be willing to admit that you have a lot to learn from experienced teachers. There is no shame in asking for help. Fellow teachers, parents, school volunteers, friends, and even students can be a time-saving resource for your classroom, but only if you take the time to ask them.

- **Get to *really* know your principal.** Look for principals to spend time with you, visiting your classroom, and looking at your lesson plans. This is a routine part of relationship building and should not be threatening in any way. Your principal is always available for individual conferences.

- **Expect it to take a lot of work.** You will be assuming the full load of an experienced educator, but you will be doing it without the benefit of the experience. There is much to learn and some of the "lessons" are easier than others. Just remember that as your experience and skills grow, so will your ability to work efficiently and effectively. If educating early adolescents were simple, it wouldn't be a profession!

- **Don't try to do it all now.** No matter how experienced any of us becomes, we find that the work is *never* done. Don't sweat the small stuff! In teaching, perhaps more than in any other profession, we really must put things into proper perspective. I hardly think anyone will really care if the bulletin board border is slightly torn! You are probably the only one who noticed. Plain old scissors do just fine. You don't need the ones which cut pretty patterns on all edges of everything they touch. Focus on those things which are truly important. Let's face it, we are there to teach children.

Many of the things we worry about don't fall into the teaching-learning category, so they may just not be worth a disproportionate amount of time, effort, and lost sleep. It is not possible to do enough for the children about whom we all care so much. The most important things are: to care about your students and your professional colleagues, to stay involved in your school, and to stay informed and on track with curriculum priorities.

- **Be flexible and willing to adapt to new situations.** Rigidity wins battles, but loses wars and friends.
- **Be yourself.** Your school hired you because they like you.

adapted from http://www.teachermentors.com
(Barry Sweeny, Best Practice Resources)

Prepare Your Classroom Management System

A solid classroom management approach is key to a good school year. Begin the first day with your plan in place. If your school is using a school-wide behavior management program (e.g., CHAMPs, or Harry Wong-based routines and procedures) you will be trained before you begin. Implement the school-wide approach if one is in place. If there is no school-wide approach, develop your own. It may help to keep the following guidelines in mind:

1. Be sure you know, and are prepared to enforce, any school-wide expectations for behavior in common areas—hallways, cafeteria, playing fields, etc.

2. Develop classroom rules consistent with school rules and which administrators will support. Rules need to be within student control to accomplish, limited in number, and clear and specific about observable behaviors.

3. Establish routines and procedures to handle daily classroom needs such as:
   - use of restrooms
   - beginning and ending of class (expectations concerning

attendance, noise, seating, and dismissal)
- handing out and collecting materials, papers, and equipment
- movement within the classroom

4. Accompanying your classroom expectations should be a set of consequences.

5. Remember . . . the overuse of punishments decreases effectiveness, and can actually be reinforcing to the child who craves attention.

6. Plan the layout of your classroom to reduce traffic flow problems, keep all areas visible to the teacher, and make sure as the teacher you are visible to the students.

7. Make displays, instructional areas, and clocks visible in all work areas.

8. Classroom rules should be written, posted, and enforceable.

9. Teach the students the routines and procedures. Explain what you expect in terms of "looks like" and "sounds like."

Teaching a Management Procedure Until It Becomes a Routine

1. Outline the procedure on the board or overhead.
2. Have a volunteer student read the procedure out loud.
3. Explain why it is important for everyone to follow the directions.
4. Question students for understanding.
5. Ask what the procedure looks like and sounds like.
6. Following the lesson, practice the procedure.
7. Provide specific feedback to the class on how well they have done.
8. Review the directions periodically, especially after breaks such as holidays and spring vacation.

Getting Off on the Right Foot: Part 1

10. Try to solve your own problems. Many times inappropriate behaviors can be managed easily through minor interventions. Try these minor interventions:

    - Use eye contact.
    - Practice proximity.
    - Give a silent signal.
    - Redirect behavior.
    - Issue a reminder.
    - Give a calm, assertive statement which tells the student to stop the behavior.
    - Get the activity moving.
    - Ignore the behavior.
    - Use your sense of humor.
    - Use positive reinforcement—catch them being good!

Prepare Your Classroom

Starting the school year off right sets the tone for the entire year. Great middle school teachers make sure the classroom is a place that emphasizes the culture of adolescents. The goal for any middle level teacher is to have a classroom setting that allows for student work, teacher expression, and creative use of overall space. Your classroom will be your home away from home for at least the next nine months. It helps if your space reflects your personality, your educational philosophy, and your attitude toward students. There are many ways to do that.

Start with a clean canvas.

Rick Wormeli (in his new book, *Day One and Beyond, Practical Matters for New Middle School Teachers*) and Jack Berckemeyer of the National Middle School Association suggest that you take a few extra minutes to remove everything from the room and start fresh. Remove all obstacles. Removing all of the desks, chairs, and shelves might cause the custodian to raise an eyebrow, so a warning sign to let them know that you will be giving your room a facelift is a good idea. As you think about the classroom setting, consider different seating arrangements, the placement of your desk, and the overall workspace for your students. Many sample seating plans are available on the Web.

Think differently about the classroom. The front of the room does not always have to be the front of the room! The learning environment should be designed according to learning objectives and desired outcomes, not just habit or a janitor's best guess. The key to success is your ability to get to every child to offer help with a minimum of movement and inconvenience to other students. Assign seats, at least initially. This will help you learn student names and maintain classroom control.

Decide on a seating arrangement.

(adapted from *Getting Started: A Guide for Beginning College Instructors*, University Division, Indiana University.)

A Traditional Classroom

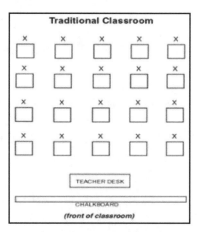

A traditional classroom is often set with the desks in rows, the teacher's desk or table somewhere in front of the room, and student desks moved far enough apart to prevent easy wandering of eyes during tests. This arrangement packs desks into the room efficiently and lets students have easy access to their seats, but it certainly does not have to be the default room arrangement. However, this arrangement is probably the best for controlling behavior, ensuring that there is space for you to walk, preventing cheating on traditional testing days. In this arrangement the role of the teacher is that of a policeman.

Two Sides Facing One Another (Bicameral)

Discussions, debates, and many other interactive classroom activities, where the whole class is looking and listening and contributing, probably work better if the students' seats are somehow facing each other. Some teachers find that this arrangement of two sides with an aisle down the middle (like Congress) works well. Put the teacher's desk in the back of the room to get it out of the way. It's still within easy access to grab a stack of handouts or other supplies. In this configuration the role of the teacher is kind of like Speaker of the House.

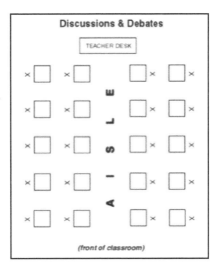

Variation: Horseshoe

A variation on the bicameral arrangement is the horseshoe. Remember, though, every arrangement should be made based on what you want the lesson to accomplish. Both the bicameral and horseshoe arrangements work well for handing out materials. The role of the teacher seems to be coordinator and collaborator in these classrooms.

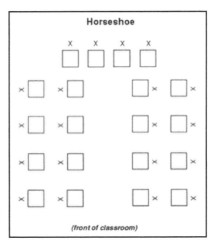

Centers

If students need to work with more materials than will fit on their desks, or with shared materials, a room arrangement of centers is a good option. You can set up the various centers around the periphery of the room while allowing space for students to get back to their desks if necessary. In this model, the students should be able to complete the center activities mostly on their own while the teacher circulates to troubleshoot and observe.

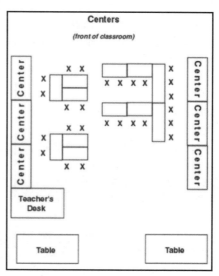

Have a plan for the first day.

There are several different ways you can have students take their seats when they first arrive in your class.

1. **Allow students to choose their own seat.**

   PRO: Doesn't require prior planning on the part of the teacher.

   CON: Students will most likely sit next to friends, which can cause early talking/disruption problems.

2. **Alphabetize students.**

   PRO: Will help you remember student names.

   CON: There will be much chaos and confusion in the classroom while you "re-seat" students once they've entered the room.

3. Use a random seating arrangement.

PRO: This is a great way for the teacher to meet each and every student as they enter the room.

CON: It does take some time to write student names into a seating chart.

Tips for Making Seating Charts:

- Design "master" seating charts that show both desk and table seating arrangements in the room. Make several copies of this sheet so that you don't have to redraw it each time you make changes.

- Use pencil when writing in student names on the seating chart to help make changes easier.

- Staple your seating chart to the right side of a manila folder for each class. On the left side you can staple a copy of your attendance sheet. Now you can check attendance without ever calling roll. Simply look at who is missing on the seating chart and record it on the roll sheet.

- To seat students randomly, use laminated colored squares. Label each table or row of desks with a different color. When greeting students at the door, have them draw a colored square from a jar or basket. Next ask them to choose a seat at the matching table or row. You can also use die-cut shapes or suites of cards.

from: *www.inspiringteachers.com/tips/firstday/index.html*

Most of your bulletin board space should be reserved to display student work. Some boards may reinforce content which is being taught. At least one area should be devoted to a copy of the class agenda. You may also want to add a small autobiographical bulletin board about yourself. This can make a powerful connection with middle level students and

Prepare bulletin boards.

will allow them to see you as a person. For more bulletin board ideas, check out these Web sites:

(http://my.att.net/p/s/community.dll?ep=16&groupid=20303&ck=)

Classroom Displays and Bulletin Boards Barbara Colvin has gathered dozens of ideas for bulletin boards, including patriotic, motivational, end-of-year, holiday, and reading bulletin boards.

(www.musicbulletinboards.net/)

Bulletin Boards for the Music Classroom After vainly searching the Net for bulletin board ideas for her K-12 music classroom, teacher Tracy King created this resource, which includes music-awareness bulletin boards, seasonal bulletin boards, and "bulletin boards that brag on your students."

(www.theteacherscorner.net/bulletinboards/index.htm)

Bulletin Board Ideas Ideas for monthly bulletin boards, subject bulletin boards, and theme boards (including good work and motivational bulletin boards) are part of this Web page from the Web site The Teacher's Corner.

Lifesavers are those little neat ideas you will pick up over time from other teachers. For example:

Learn to love "lifesavers."

Label everything. Put your name on your materials and supplies. This helps when the items turn up somewhere else in the building . . . and they will, eventually.

Photos of students help with seating charts and substitute teachers. Take a photo of each student at the beginning of the year and use it throughout the year in many ways.

Prepare a "Visual Voyage."

Jack Berckemeyer reminds us that, "When adolescents take a visual voyage (daydream) beyond your lesson, they tend to look around the room and check out the posters, books, and other visual aides that line the classroom." A middle school classroom should, therefore, be a "visual wonderland" filled with student work, appropriate pop culture posters, signs, and phrases. These send positive messages to adolescents.

There will be times when special supplies are needed, or when a student may be without routine needs. Expect this and plan for it. A word of advice from one who knows—collect end of the year goodies! On your last day with students, when they are busy cleaning out lockers and returning books, let them know that you will be happy to take them. With careful storage you should have plenty on hand for use as "loaners" next year!

Obtain student supplies.

Obtain teacher supplies.

Find out how to get transparency film and copy paper, and how to make copies. Among other things, you will probably need pens and markers, a stapler and staples, paper clips, tape, rubber bands, hall passes, and routinely-needed forms. For your own classroom tools you really should have the following:

- a stamp with your name on it, and a stamp pad (for the top of books, back of posters before you laminate, etc.)
- Tacky Finger
- a three-hole punch
- colored chalk—great for highlighting
- extra overhead projector pens
- really good scissors
- WD 40™

- Post-it™ notes of various sizes
- extremely large paper clips (so you can clip a class set of papers together)
- a white twin-size flat sheet (an instant, mobile, extra projector screen)
- a door stop (with your name on it)
- extension cord and extra surge protector
- electric pencil sharpener

Post classroom information.

Post your name, room number, and the grade and subject you teach, both inside and outside the room. If you have a telephone inside your room, post important school numbers next to the phone. Include the main office, attendance clerk, and nearby classrooms.

Look over your first day's lesson plans and make sure you have all needed material ready.

Review lesson plans.

Prepare materials for first day.

Materials your students need to take home the first day might include emergency data cards, a school/team welcome letter, a calendar showing class schedule and schedule of coming events, a class syllabus, and a homework assignment.

Start the habit of reading aloud to your students for a few minutes each day, whatever their grade level. This may be the only opportunity they have to hear fluent reading.

Check out books from the school or public library.

Do everything in pencil the first couple of weeks.

No matter what grade you teach, most likely you will have students leave and enter your classroom during the first several days. Enter student names on roll sheets, locker and textbook records, grade book, and seating chart in pencil so that you can make changes more easily and keep everything looking neat.

Prepare for the Young Adolescent

MIDDLE SCHOOL MATTERS

(a song by Mark Meckel / Monte Selby)

Alarm beeps too early
Straight hair, want it curly
Clothes fittin' too small
Out of style, shoppin' mall
Takes it all, no money
Daddy laughs, ain't funny
Takes a kid's point of view
It ain't easy gettin' through
Tired of hearing it's a phase
Someday ain't today
Who cares anyway?
School's out, next May
Every day a little change
A little good, a little strange
Hopin' for a little luck
Want a car, want a truck
They say you ain't old enough
All part of growing up
Plan a future don't look back
Hurry, do your homework fast
Can't figure out the math
Turn into a psychopath
Sit in class
Laying low
Hope the teacher
    doesn't know

CHORUS:
  Middle school matters
  Middle school matters
  It matters if you happen
  to be that
  middle school kid

No excuse, no denial
Got in trouble, on trial
Just keep puttin' on the
brakes
But, everybody makes
mistakes
Not sure what's next
Can't find it in the text
Voice cracks
Time to sing
Wanna dance to wild thing
Wrong food, deep fried
Get zits, wanna hide
Look harder, gotta find
A good person deep inside

CHORUS

So, take a look, take a listen
Don't wait, time's tickin'
Parent, teacher, grandma
Cousin, uncle, step-mom
Notice every smile, frown
Acting up, helping out
Good day, bad week
Need a ton of relief
Made it worse than it is
Can't help it, need a friend
Principal or secretary
More love, less scary

CHORUS

Prepare to Meet the Middle School Student

The middle school student is an early adolescent. This is a challenging, yet exciting, age to teach. It helps if you know what to expect on day one.

• Cognitively . . .

- Some of your students are ready for abstract thinking, some are not.

- Some of your students think abstractly in one subject, but not in another.

- All of your students are intensely curious and growing in mental abilities.

- They prefer active learning, especially when incorporated with interaction with others.

- They enjoy games, puzzles, riddles, and using skills to solve real-life problems.

- They become increasingly independent and think more critically as the year progresses.

• Socially . . .

- Middle schoolers model themselves after their peers rather than their families.

- They adopt fads in speech, clothing, mannerisms, and handwriting.

- They are lost in a maze of longing for direction at the same time that they are questioning authority.

- They sometimes show erratic, unusual, or bizarre behavior.

- They show extreme devotion to friends and romantic interests, but may transfer allegiances overnight.

- They feel the will of the group must come first, often being cruel to those not in the group.

• Emotionally . . .

– Early adolescents often become agitated with too-rapid or too-slow physical development.

– They are fearful of things real and imagined, but compensate with bravado.

– They sometimes regress to childlike behavior.

– They are easily offended and are supersensitive to criticism.

– They lack self-confidence.

– They sometimes tend to exaggerate.

• Physically . . .

– Many lack coordination and move awkwardly.

– They feel unlimited energy, but seem to tire easily.

– They are self-conscious, and worry about body

changes and physical appearance.

– They have ravenous appetites and peculiar tastes.

– Male development tends to lag behind female.

adapted from "The Essential Middle School." Jon Wiles and Joseph Bondi

Prepare Daily Lesson Plans

All lessons are based on curriculum, that is, what students are intended to learn. Lesson plans are written by teachers to help structure the intended learning for **themselves** as well as for the students. There are many ways to write and structure lesson plans.

Lesson plans are not written for teachers to read to the class. They help with the flow of the class, especially when something has happened to distract everyone, including the teacher. What follows is a sample for your consideration.

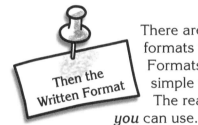

First, the Thinking

Lesson planning is a thinking process and is basically completed in four parts.

1. First, determine the curriculum goal (the core content for assessment); that is, what the students will learn, and what students will be able to do upon completing the activities or work of the lesson.

2. Before beginning the lesson, determine what the students already know that provides a base and can lead to the new content.

3. Determine at least one way to assist the students in learning the new curriculum.

4. Determine at least one way to evaluate (assess) students' learning outcomes.

Then the Written Format

There are any number of perfectly good formats to use to write daily lesson plans. Formats that are the most useful are very simple to follow and are well-structured. The real trick is to find a lesson plan format *you* can use.

On page 93 is a sample of one type of outline format.

Lesson plans can include many additional components such as materials needed, assessments, evaluation procedures, etc. The outline presented here is meant to be a quick and efficient, but highly effective, way to develop daily lesson plans. You will need to complete the thinking and mental structuring of the lesson before beginning the written format.

Time-Saving Tip

Save time writing out detailed lesson plans by using the computer. Create a template for a week's worth of plans and save it as "template." Be sure to include your daily routines in the template so that all you have to do is change the daily objectives and a few specific procedures for each individual lesson. When it is time to write your plans for the next week, pull up the template and save as "week ___." This saves time in the long run when you don't have to write the same details over and over again! Another way this saves time is when you have a substitute. If you already have detailed lesson plans ready, there will be no need to write out a separate set of plans for the sub!

adapted from Dr. Sandra Kizlik. Adprima.com

Plan to Include ALL CHILDREN in Your Lesson Plans: Learning Activities for the Seven Intelligences

It is important, when teaching young adolescents, to give them a variety of activities. All students learn in a variety of ways and every child has one or more strengths and one or more weaknesses. By planning classroom activities that utilize the different learning styles and learning intelligences, we are giving students both a chance to be successful and a chance to meet challenges.

For the student who is a verbal/linguistic learner, journal writing is a joy, but when it is time for computation games, that same student may be at a loss. This does not mean that we only teach to the particular student's learning style or intelligence, but rather that by touching upon all of them we can help each and every one of our students be comfortable with ALL of the learning styles and intelligences! Use the following list of activities to help you plan to meet the needs of ALL of your students!

VERBAL/LINGUISTIC LEARNERS:

enjoy activities that involve reading, writing, and speaking.

writing workshop
journals; diaries
debating
literature circles
creative writing
poetry
teaching others
humor
jokes
readers' theater
storytelling
alphabetizing; dictionaries
classroom newsletters
interviews
class discussions
library visits
vocabulary games

VISUAL/SPATIAL LEARNERS:

enjoy learning through visualizing, diagrams, and a range of visual media.

illustrating info.
filmmaking
mapmaking
murals
designing posters
graphs; flow charts
observations
sewing; beading; weaving
geometrical building
woodworking
chess
cartoons
using symbols
sculpting; painting; drawing
guided imagery
webbing; mapping
visual languages; signing
collages

LOGICAL/ MATHEMATICAL LEARNERS:

enjoy working with numbers, experimenting, patterning, and asking questions.

predicting; estimating
conducting surveys
brain teasers
statistics
sequencing; timelines
puzzles; kits
graphing info.
probability
following recipes
codes
Venn diagrams
research projects
computation games
computers; calculators
measuring
creating games; programs
scientific experiments

BODILY/ KINESTHETIC LEARNERS:

enjoy activities that allow them to move, touch, and do.

block building
scavenger hunts
crafts
sculpting
Playdough™
performing
demonstrating
acting out
building/designing
science experiments
charades
presentations
movement games

Prepare an Atmosphere of Positive Expectations: The Key to Supporting Social and Emotional Intelligence

Many middle level schools have not developed a formal program designed to support social and emotional learning. But, there are many easy activities and practices you can initiate in your own classroom that will fill that void.

One factor which can mean the difference between students who succeed at high levels and those who merely get by is the degree to which teachers create an environment of high positive expectations. Positive expectations are not equivalent to high standards. Standards are levels of achievement. However, teachers who practice positive expectations will help students reach higher standards because students tend to achieve to the degree to which they perceive teachers believe they can. There are many ways to create an atmosphere of high positive expectations for all students. The list which follows is merely a sampling.

- **Dress for success.** When we come to school dressed as professionals, we convey our belief that our students are important and we want to look good for them. Students feel valued. The way we dress affects both the work attitude and discipline of our students. In addition, by dressing professionally, we gain the respect, credibility, acceptance, and authority that we might otherwise have trouble getting.

- **Welcome students as they enter your classroom.** Always smile. As you become familiar with each one, greet them by name and acknowledge something special about each one.

- **Learn student names as quickly as possible.** Our name is our identity. To call a person by name is to acknowledge him as a worthy individual. Using a student's name often, shows that you care.

- **Take advantage of positive verbal comments.** Try to use at least three positive comments for every negative. Even comments like "Good Morning," "I appreciate your help," and "How may I help you?" can have a very positive effect.

- **Show respect by using positive body language.** Smile, listen, hold the door, wait your turn.

- **Encourage and model positive habits.** Courtesy and respect should be part of the expected verbiage in every classroom. Modeling our expectations lets students know what to do and implies that we believe they can do it.

- **Create a positive classroom environment.** Fresh live plants, clean walls, displayed student work, and fresh air all indicate that we respect and value our students.

- **If your school does not have an advisory program, institute morning meetings.** Starting your day as a community provides multiple opportunities to support social and emotional learning. It helps build a positive sense of community, creates a climate of trust, and encourages respectful communication.

- **Emphasize the positive nature of responsibility.** Create formal tasks in your classroom like cleaning the boards, taking papers to the office, handing out and collecting material or supplies. Appoint a class librarian to assist you with your classroom library. Such tasks can be effective ways of positively encouraging a sense of responsibility among all of your students. It also feels very democratic to the whole class.

- **Encourage creativity.** Joshua Freedman, director of programs for Six Seconds, a nonprofit organization supporting emotional intelligence in families, schools, corporations, and communities, suggests that creativity is most necessary in times of emotional hardship, such as when we are frustrated or angry. This is especially true of the middle school student. By providing your students with ongoing opportunities to express their creativity, you will also be helping them handle the inevitable curve balls that life throws at them.

BEAT OF A DIFFERENT MARCHER

(A Song by Monte Selby / Debbie Silver)

Bobby marches to the beat of his different drummers
Jeffery does his reading, but he can't do numbers
Shauna's up and talking ninety miles an hour again
Can't find his book or pencil, that would be Ben
Hyperactive, dyslexic, class clown, non-reader
Upper-class, no-class, off task, bottom feeder
Little Artie's a challenge, Martin's a dream
We've seen them all, they all need to be seen

CHORUS

All children in reach, when we find their rhythm
The step, the dance, the song within them
That's a better journey, but so much harder
Too extraordinary, but so much smarter
To drum to the beat of each different marcher

Sandy's in the slow group, a proven low achiever
She's the small quiet one, not a class leader
With crayons in her hand, she can draw what she knows best
But no room for pictures on the standardized test
Ballerina, bricklayer, biochemist, ballplayer
Diesel driver, drum major, diva destined, dragon slayer
Some kids have a chance with a different choice
To show what they know, they must have a voice

CHORUS

Introspective, oversized, minimized, criticized
Round holes, square lives, not much room for compromise
There's a new song not yet written for each and every child
Will we listen?

CHORUS

Getting Off on the Right Foot: Part 2

Day One: Jump In with Both Feet!

- Arrive early! Give the classroom one last check.

- Greet the students at the door.
Introduce yourself and welcome them.
Don't wait until after Christmas to smile!

- As students arrive, hand them an assignment
and ask them to get started immediately.
A student data sheet is included in this
booklet (reproducible copy on page 94)
as an example of a good opening assignment.
This not only provides the teacher with
necessary data, but also gives some insight
into the student's thinking and behavior.

   The back of each student's data sheet may be used to
   record any communication with the home throughout
   the year. Three-hole punched, and kept in a binder,
   these sheets are a valuable record.

- Begin to develop your learning community. It is important
for you to know each student and for the students to know
each other. Develop an age-appropriate activity to ensure
that names are learned on the first day of class.

- Review, explain, and discuss school rules and procedures.

- Work together to develop a list of classroom rules and
consequences.

- As you move throughout the day, explain and practice
classroom procedures.

- Take pictures of students at work and at play. Save some
for Parents' Night (Open House) and for student-of-the-
week bulletin boards. Use others to start a class scrapbook.

- Give out classroom jobs, for example:

   Classroom Greeter—Keep a basket full of useful items
   such as breath mints, bookmarks, fancy paper, pens,

Post-It™ notes, etc. for anyone who might visit your room. A student in charge of this job would greet visitors at the door and present them with a gift. Teach the students how to properly greet visitors, address them politely, and invite them to observe. Later, the greeter writes a "Thank You For Visiting Our Class . . . Come Again" card. The greeter can be a helpful guide for new students who enter in the middle of the year.

Classroom Photographer—Keep a camera (digital or disposable) in class, and when you are doing an especially interesting activity, simulation, or experiment the student photographer can record the events. When the pictures are printed, the photographer writes captions for the pictures and posts them on a bulletin board with a short news report of the event.

Door Decorator—A student is in charge of decorating the door monthly with all homeroom students' names, and may include a topic or theme that is being studied (or, it can just be fun). Be sure to give the student examples and materials.

adapted from www.edu-cyberpg.com/Teachers/newteacherkit.html

- **Congratulate yourself on a job well done!**

Prepare to Praise Students
Ways to Praise:

Use the following phrases along with a specific statement of what the student did well:

(For example: Wow! I love how you and Amy worked together until you got the assignment done. Good job!)

Wow! Terrific! That's great! Fantastic! Superb! Good job! Nice going! Awesome! Good try! Excellent! I appreciate . . . ! You're tops! Hurray! Way to go! Keep it up! Great effort! You're doing fine! Thank you! Doing good!

Smile, shake hands, thumbs up, high five

from: Lee Canter and Associates, 1992

Praise students for:

- entering the classroom quietly
- arriving at class on time
- cooperating while teacher takes attendance
- returning permission slips and school forms on time
- transitioning into an activity
- following directions
- saying "please" and "thank you"
- listening attentively
- helping a classmate
- bringing necessary materials to class
- handing in homework
- being a polite audience at an assembly
- beginning work right away
- asking questions when unsure
- good behavior during a test
- participating in a class discussion
- walking appropriately in the halls
- working cooperatively with a partner
- a performance in a play or presentation
- cleaning up
- good effort on an assignment
- assisting a new student
- sharing school experiences with parents
- making up missed assignments
- making a new friend
- sharing
- learning a new skill
- good effort on a long-term project
- being sensitive to others' feelings
- appropriate use of school property
- returning borrowed books & materials
- showing enthusiasm
- being responsible for a classroom job
- offering help without being asked
- not wasting paper and supplies
- staying on task
- telling the truth
- accepting a new challenge
- behaving when a guest is in the room
- reading at home
- participating in school functions
- demonstrating a positive attitude
- giving one's best effort
- participating in a community improvement project
- participating in a group activity
- remaining calm during a problem situation
- showing creativity
- keeping busy when work is finished
- taking turns
- working cooperatively with an aide or volunteer

Getting Off on the Right Foot: Part 2

The Age of Caterpillars:
A Time to Learn to Fly

(a middle school teacher's story)
by Dave Puckett

I sat, today,
In the warming glow
Of the morning sun,
Doing the unexpected . . .
    Watching a fuzz-adorned,
    Yellow and green and black caterpillar
    Making what I suppose could be called . . . progress,
    In his struggle to cross the vast expanse of the walkway
    In my rose garden.
    He . . . (At least I think it was a he
      How does anyone tell for sure
      at that caterpillar stage?) . . .
    Wiggled his baby fat, bulbous body
    On many unsure feet,
As he fretted and squiggled
To get wherever it was he was going.
    Throughout the process,
    He looked puzzled
    As only a caterpillar can look . . .
    Sort of dazed . . .
    Apathetic . . .
    But yet
    Pathetically puzzled,
    As though he weren't sure
    Where he was going . . .
    Or how he was going to get there . . .
    Or how he would be sure where he was
    When he did get there.
    But, on he went . . .

And went . . .
And went.
I thought to myself,
How do caterpillars ever learn to fly?
At what point do they decide to sprout wings?
Are they born with flight as an ultimate goal?
Or, does it all come as a serendipitous surprise?
I'm not sure.
The only thing I am sure of,
As I sit here in the sun,
A mere spectator in the process,
Is that, given the right environment,
Nurtured by lush foliage and warm sunshine,
Protected from predatory beasts,
And provided with time . . . his own time . . .
Caterpillar time . . .
He will learn to fly!
What I most need to remember is
That in my haste and hurry to see him be
    The butterfly he is destined to become,
    I do not become so hasty and harsh
    In my concern for his progress
That I push too hard, and step too fast, and crush him
    just as he is about to cross the threshold of my garden gate.

PART 3

Prepare to Work With Parents

LETTER TO ANDY'S TEACHER
(a song by Monte Selby / John Tirro)

This is my son
His name's Andy
He likes bikes and peanut butter
He reads well for someone his age
He has lots of jokes to tell you
But, sometimes he dreams
At the wrong times
And sometimes, this seems to be a problem
As his teacher, please remember
Everybody learns things differently

2002 Street Singer Music, BMI/Mondo Zen Music, ASCAP

Prepare for Your Students' Parents

Establishing rapport and a cooperative working relationship with parents is essential for any teacher, but is especially important to the first-year teacher, whose inexperience may be an issue for some parents. A welcome letter will help you get off on the right foot. If possible, mail the letters a week or two before the opening of school. If that isn't possible, send it home with students on the first day. Include information about yourself, your class, and any special supplies the student may need. You may also want to take the opportunity to encourage parent volunteerism. Be sure your principal, mentor-teacher, or another veteran teacher reviews the parent letters before you mail them. They know the community and school policies better than you do and are in a better position to evaluate whether the letter is effective and appropriate.

adapted from: Linda Starr, *Education World*, 2001

Look to Parents to . . .

- Show support for learning at home
- Communicate positive feedback about a teacher's influence or performance
- Welcome new teachers
- Volunteer to help in the classroom
- Support fair discipline measures that teachers impose
- Refrain from assuming the worst about first-year teachers
- See their children do their homework
- Offer their workplace for a field trip when appropriate
- Talk to a teacher directly about a problem
- Become active partners in education

Tips for Working with Parents

- Contact parents early on, before a problem occurs, particularly when there is good news to report.
- Consider writing a weekly newsletter or report on classroom learning and activities.
- Invite parents to come into the classroom and assign tasks if they are willing.
- Involve them in reading groups when possible, being aware that parents may not read or write English.
- Let parents know that they can reinforce classroom learning at home.
- Address parents' concerns head-on.

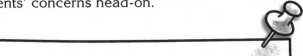

NOTE: Making Newsletters Easier

- Create a template on the computer that you can use over and over.
- Use the cut-and-paste feature of the computer to cut out unwanted information and insert new events and information.
- Keep the sections the same for each newsletter so that you don't have to make it up from scratch each time. Possible sections might include:

  —Upcoming topics, concepts, and/or units being taught

  —Birthdays

  —Thank-you section for parents, students, and volunteers

  —Field trips/special events

  —Activities to do with students at home

  —New teaching/ learning strategies (By including a section that explains the latest teaching/learning techniques and theories, you can help parents understand why your classroom may be different from one they are used to.)

  —Test-taking skills to practice at home

  —Critical-thinking skills

Telephone Calls to Parents

Don't let the large number of students you teach deter you from making positive contact with parents. Planning well will help you establish contact with every parent. You'll be surprised at the number of students you can reach if you simply schedule time for positives. A quick positive phone call takes only a couple of minutes. Start on the first Monday of school, make two brief calls each afternoon, and you will reach ten parents each week. Multiply by 36 weeks, and you will reach 360 parents. Think about when you could schedule time for calls each week. Then set a goal of speaking with a specific number of parents each week.

adapted from: *First-Class Teacher: Success Strategies for New Teachers.*
Canter and Associates. 1998.

Opportunities for Positive Phone Calls

- Before the first day of the school year, call to introduce yourself, express enthusiasm about your plans for the class, and ask for information about the student.

- Call when a student demonstrates a positive behavior, such as befriending a new student or helping you clean up the classroom before or after school.

- Call when a student applies himself or herself to an especially challenging task.

- Call when a student who has had difficulty in one area shows improvement.

- Call when a student is absent for more than a day or two, to say that the class missed him and to see whether the student needs work sent home.

Prepare for Open House

Display student work around the room and in the hallways for parents to view.

Parents may or may not look at the work depending on their schedule. You may need to point out the work displayed and encourage your students to show their parents around.

Be prepared to explain your classroom policies & procedures.

Generally, middle schools have the parents follow their child's class schedule. Each session will last no more than 20 minutes. You will have one or two sessions with no parents due to your planning and team time. Use this time to catch up on work, or check out the Teacher's Lounge and see if there are any treats waiting!

Make your talk fun and interesting.

Your parents have worked all day, too. The last thing they want is to be TALKED AT by some teacher. Give them the information with some humor! Have a few teaching cartoons displayed on the overhead.

Have your information typed out for parents to take home!

Instead of speed-talking your way through your classroom expectations, procedures, upcoming units, field trips, etc., type it out for your parents to take home! Highlight a few things in your speech, then encourage parents to read the rest when they get home.

Prepare for Parent Conferences

Parent conferences are essential and, quite frankly, inevitable. In many school districts, they are expected for all students, good and less-than-good alike. The National Education Association offers several helpful hints for holding successful parent conferences. Among them are:

- *Invite both parents.* Be flexible, remembering that many families today are non-traditional families. Encourage both parents and adult guardians to attend conferences when possible. Misunderstandings are less common if all concerned adults hear what you have to say, and you'll be able to gauge the kind of support the child receives. Of course, remember that all parties may not be available. Try to schedule conferences at a time when parents and family members are available.

- *Make contact early.* You'll get your relationship with parents off to a good start if you contact them early in the year, perhaps with a memo or newsletter sent home to all pupils. Give parents an outline of what their children will be studying, and let them know you'll be happy to meet with them during the year. (Be sure to say how and when they may contact you for conferences.)

- *Allow enough time.* Schedule plenty of time for the meeting. Twenty to thirty minutes is usually adequate. If you're scheduling back-to-back conferences, be sure to allow enough time between them (ten minutes or so) so you can make necessary notes on the just-concluded conference and prepare for the upcoming one.

- *Be ready for questions.* Be prepared to answer specific questions parents may have. They're likely to ask questions such as:
  - What is my child's ability level?
  - Is my child working up to his/her ability level?
  - How is my child doing in specific subjects?
  - Does my child cause any trouble?
  - Does my child have any specific skills or abilities in schoolwork?

Getting Off on the Right Foot: Part 3

- ***Get your papers organized in advance.*** Assemble your grade book, test papers, samples of the student's work, attendance records, and other pertinent data together ahead of time. That way you won't be fumbling through stacks on your desk during the meeting.

- ***Plan ahead.*** Have in mind a general but flexible outline of what you're going to say, including a survey of student progress, a review of his or her strengths and needs, and a proposed plan of action.

- ***Greet parents near the entrance they'll use.*** You'll alleviate anxiety and frustration (nothing is more confusing to the uninitiated than wandering around those look-alike school hallways trying to find the right classroom) and make parents feel more welcome.

- ***Get the name right.*** Don't assume that Jennifer Peabody's mother is Mrs. Peabody. She could well have been married again since Jennifer was born. Check your records ahead of time to make sure you've got the parents' names right. And don't assume that the wrinkled gray-haired gentleman coming in with Johnny is his grandfather. It could be his father, or an uncle. Politely ask. Try not to talk to the Smiths about their son "Stan" when their son's name is "Steve."

- ***Avoid physical barriers.*** Don't sit behind your desk, while forcing the parents to squeeze into the children's desks on the front row or perch miserably on folding chairs. Arrange a conference-style seating if possible so you'll all be equals together.

- ***Open on a positive note.*** Begin conferences on a warm, positive note to get everyone relaxed. Start with a positive statement about the child's abilities, work, or interests.

- ***Structure the session.*** As soon as the parents arrive, review the structure of the conference—the why, what, how, and when—so that you'll both have an agenda.

- ***Be specific in your comments.*** Parents may flounder if you deal only in generalities. Instead of saying, "She doesn't accept responsibility," pin down the problem by pointing out, "Amanda had a whole week to finish her report but she wrote only two paragraphs."

- *Offer a suggested course of action.* Parents appreciate being given some specific direction. If Jane is immature, it might be helpful to suggest parents give her a list of weekly chores, allow her to take care of a pet, or give her a notebook to write down assignments. (Of course, when you offer advice, let parents know you're only making a suggestion.)

- *Forget the jargon.* Education jargon phrases like "criterion-referenced testing," "perceptual skills," and "least restrictive environment" may be just too much double-talk to many parents.

- *Turn the other cheek.* In routine parent conferences, it's unusual to run into parents who are abusive and hostile. But it can happen. Try to not be rude, whatever the provocation. Hear out the parents in as pleasant a manner as possible, without getting defensive if you can.

- *Ask for parents' opinions.* Let parents know you're interested in their opinions, are eager to answer their questions, and want to work with them throughout the year to help make their child's education the best.

- *Focus on strengths.* It's very easy for parents to feel defensive since many of them see themselves in their children. You'll help if you review the child's strengths and areas of need rather than dwelling on criticism or stressing weaknesses.

- *Use body language.* Nonverbal cues set the mood of the conference. Smile, nod, make eye contact, and lean forward slightly. You'll be using your body language to let parents know you're interested and approving.

- *Stress collaboration.* Let the parent know you want to work together in the best interests of the child. A statement such as, "You need to see me as soon as possible to discuss Johnny's poor study habits" only arouses hostility, while, "I'd like to discuss with you how we might work together to improve Johnny's study habits" gets the relationship off on the right foot.

- *Listen to what parents say.* Despite the fact that we spend nearly a third of our lives listening, most adults are poor listeners. We concentrate on what we're going to say next, or we let our minds drift off to other concerns, or we hear only part of what a speaker is saying. You'll get more out of a parent conference if you really listen to what parents are saying to you.

- *Ask about the child.* You don't want to pry, of course, but remember to ask the parents if there's anything they think you should know about the child (such as study habits, relationship with siblings, any important events in his or her life) which may affect his or her school work.

- *Focus on solutions.* Ideally all parent conferences would concern only positive events. Realistically, many conferences are held because there's a problem somewhere. Things will go more smoothly if you focus on solutions rather than on the child's problem. Discuss what you and the parents can do to help improve the situation. Plan a course of action together.

- *Don't judge.* It may not always be possible to react neutrally to what parents say, but communicating your judgments of parents' behaviors can be a roadblock to a productive relationship with them.

- *Summarize.* Before the conference ends, summarize the discussion and what actions you and the parents have decided to take.

- *Wind up on a positive note.* When you can, save at least one encouraging comment or positive statement about the student for the end of the conference.

- *Meet again if you need to.* If you feel you need more time, arrange another meeting later rather than trying to rush everything before the kids get back from art class.

- *Keep a record of the conference.* You may find it helpful later to have a brief record of what was said at the conference, what suggestions for improvement were made, and so forth. Make notes as soon as possible after the conference while the details are still fresh. And, as a courtesy, send a copy of the conference report to the parent.

PART 4

Prepare to Become a Professional

Prepare to Learn Your ABC's
All Over Again: Alphabet Soup for Teachers

Much of the world of education is like a bowl of alphabet soup whose letters are jumbled and meaningless. For those just entering that world, the number of acronyms may become overwhelming. To give you a head start, here are a few of the most common.

NMSA — National Middle School Association

CATS — Commonwealth Accountability Testing System

HSE — Highly Skilled Educator (assigned to schools whose CATS results indicated assistance is needed)

NCLB — No Child Left Behind (Federally mandated measures to reform education)

AYP — Adequate Yearly Progress in light of NCLB

SISI — Standards and Indicators of School Improvement

CSIP — Comprehensive School Improvement Plan (an individual school's strategic planning document)

PD — Professional Development

SBDM — Site-Based Decision Making; the school Council

TGIF — self-explanatory!

Prepare for Professional Growth and Development

Contrary to what many veteran teachers will tell you, professional development is not torture equal to any medieval stretching machine. Professional development should be a time of professional growth and continuing education. Here are a few tips to help you make your professional development experiences valuable.

1. Take the Learning into Your Own Hands.

Remember that you are the one who needs to benefit from the information being delivered. Come to the session with an open mind and a willingness to learn. Just as your students need to be open to what you teach them, so should you be open to what others have to teach you. You never know what jewel of an idea or strategy you may discover. Remember that teaching equals lifelong learning.

2. Go with a Positive Attitude.

We are always saying this to our students and it applies to us as well. If you walk into a professional development session with a poor attitude and no intention of learning anything, then you will have a wasted day. If, however, you walk in with an open mind and a positive attitude, you just may get several great ideas to use during the school year. You will get ideas, not only from the session itself, but also from casual conversations happening before, during, and after the session.

3. Encourage Others Around You to Maintain a Positive Outlook Regarding the Session.

We all know teachers who prefer to sit in the back and complain about the session before it even begins. This negative attitude can infect everyone around that person, which causes a chain reaction through the room. Instead of responding to another negative comment with a negative comment, try to infect that person with your positive attitude. You might try pointing out something positive for each negative comment. If all else fails, move to another seat so that you are not distracted.

4. Don't Bring Anything Else to Do.

Although you may run the risk of being bored, take a chance and be proactive in your learning. If you don't bring any other tasks with you to the session, you won't be tempted to start working on them while the presenter is speaking. It is difficult to listen and learn when your mind is focused on other tasks.

5. Don't Be Afraid to Ask Questions.

Go ahead and speak up. If something is confusing you, raise your hand and ask for clarification. The session will do you no good if you sit through half of it confused. Most likely if you are confused, several others are too. Also, ask for examples of how strategies presented would look in the classroom. Don't wait until the end to ask your questions, but instead ask when the question is pertinent.

6. Request Meaningful Activities and Information.

Before the session begins, speak with the presenter and request that he or she give practical ways to apply and implement the information throughout the presentation rather than only at the end or just in a handout. If you let the person in charge know what you are looking for ahead of time, he or she may be able to adapt the presentation to meet your requests.

7. Provide Specific Constructive Feedback to the Presenter.

If the session still ends up making it on your "worst" list, let those in charge know why it was a complete bust. Don't forget to start out with one or two positive comments first. Be sure to offer a couple of suggestions for correcting the problems. Sometimes those who are presenting professional development sessions forget how to be good teachers. Your comments may help someone else have a great experience. Who knows, perhaps one day you'll find yourself presenting to a group of teachers and will appreciate helpful feedback from them.

Prepare for Paperwork

Managing the paperwork is one of the toughest things a new teacher has to learn the first couple of years in the classroom. Memos, directives, staff development forms, student forms, work requests, and general FYI papers can really accumulate if they are not organized and handled with efficiency. This doesn't even take into account student work that must be graded, recorded, and passed back to students.

Tips to Help You
Keep Up with All of This Paperwork!

- As soon as you check your box in the teacher's lounge or office area, prioritize your mail. Place the high priority items that need an immediate response in front and the items that don't need immediate attention (magazines or catalogs) in the back of the pile.

- When people request a written response from you, immediately jot your response and put it in their box. Don't wait until you are back in your classroom before answering the message. Chances are it will sit on your desk for a week before getting back to the other person.

- As soon as you get back to your classroom, go through your mail before doing anything else.

- After reading a memo, write down important dates and times on your desk calendar (be sure to include a few specifics as well as the contact person). Then throw the memo away or file it in your teacher binder (chronologically for easy reference). Don't let it sit on your desk or in your calendar.

- Go ahead and fill out administrative forms (recommendations, referrals, work requests, lunch requests, etc.) and place them in a folder marked "Return to Office."

- Immediately file staff development or FYI flyers.

- Place magazines and catalogs in your bag to take home and review in the evening. Although you may be tempted to read through the magazine or catalog during your planning period, you could better spend your time getting things done! Use magazines and catalogs as bathtime or bedtime reading material.

Web Tools for Reducing Paperwork

A handful of free online tools are true lifesavers. Those tools help streamline some of the most tedious paperwork tasks that get in the way of one-on-one time with students. They help bury some of the paperwork. They help us focus on our "soul mission"—connecting with our students. Best of all, those tools enhance our instruction time by helping students reflect, organize, and think in new ways.

Learning Checklists

(http://pblchecklist.4teachers.org)

This practical learning tool scaffolds students as they learn to take responsibility for their learning. It enables teachers to create customized checklists they can print for student use.

RubiStar

(http://rubistar.4teachers.org/index.php)

Rubistar's easy-to-use template helps teachers create curriculum-specific rubrics in a minimum amount of time. The rubrics help define assignment expectations for students and they speed up the marking process for teachers.

Zoomerang

(http://www.zoomerang.com/Login/index.zgi)

This online survey tool provides a way to find out what students, parents, and peers know and think. The survey results arm educators with data to adjust and improve instruction and communication.

ThinkTank

(http://thinktank.4teachers.org)

This site offers a fun way for students to create research organizers for reports and projects. It is a great tool for guiding student thinking.

Puzzlemaker

(http://puzzlemaker.school.discovery.com/)

This practical Web site turns word lists into customized word search, crossword, and math puzzles. Puzzles can be saved in a "custom account" to be retrieved later.

iKeepBookmarks

(http://ikeepbookmarks.com/)

This site not only organizes favorite Web page bookmarks, but also creates special topical folders for students to use as they research specific topics.

The Connection Cube

(http://learnweb.harvard.edu/alps/thinking/reflect_activities.cfm#connection)

Helping students make connections between what they already know and new learning is one of the most important things teachers do. This online tool helps students connect learning to new contexts.

Teacher Forms and Letters

(http://www.teachertools.org/forms_dynam.asp)

Downloadable templates are listed in four categories: Discipline, Academic, Communication, and Other.

Prepare to Teach the Unexpected: All Teachers Teach Reading

Many school districts are placing strong emphasis on teaching reading strategies within other content classrooms. Regardless of your certification and training—social studies, math, science, language arts, or music—ALL middle school teachers teach reading. Prepare for it now. "Let's spend the next 20 minutes reading this chapter, then we'll discuss it," rarely works. The reason is simple: as students move into middle school, they begin to make the shift from "learning to read" to "reading to learn." Prior years of education have focused on learning to read *narrative* text and many students encounter difficulties when asked to read *content area* textbooks. There are several reasons for this:

- The features and structure of informational texts are unfamiliar to students.

- Students must deal with new, content-specific vocabulary.

- Prior knowledge about the content area may be shaky or nonexistent.

Research suggests that if we want to help our students become independent, strategic readers of textbooks, we need to change the format of our lessons. This diagram from *Teaching Reading in the Content Areas: If Not Me, Then Who?* by Rachel Billmeyer and Mary Lee Barton (McREL) illustrates it best:

TRADITIONAL FORMAT ➡ *Less Time*	NEW FORMAT *More Time*
Reading assignment given	Prereading activities: Discussion Predictions Questioning Brainstorming Setting purpose
Independent reading	Guided ACTIVE reading
Discussion to see if students learned main concepts, what they "should have" learned	Activities to clarify, reinforce, extend knowledge
More Time	*Less Time*

Teaching Text Structures

Most textbooks have common formatting features that students should be able to recognize. Try building a textbook scavenger hunt to help familiarize your students with textbook features such as:

Glossary	Indexes	Charts, graphs, tables
Illustrations	Captions	Review questions
Titles	Bullets	Boldface words
Headings	Sidebars	Table of contents

Model by thinking aloud how you use these features to improve your understanding of the material. Ask questions such as, "What is the author's purpose for using this feature?" or, "What main ideas does this feature illustrate?" Encourage students to look for "signal words" to determine the structure of the text. For example:

Structure	Signal Words
Cause/Effect	because, consequently, as a result of, therefore, since . . .
Compare/Contrast	on the other hand, instead of, different from, similar to . . .
Descriptive	for instance, for example, furthermore, such as, also . . .
Problem/Solution	the question is, one answer is, recommendations include . . .
Sequence/Chronological Order	first, second, initially, before, after, when, . . .

Teach students to map information using graphic organizers that match the structure of the text (e.g., Venn Diagram for compare/contrast, timeline for chronological order, flow chart for problem/solution, web for cause/effect, etc.).

Coping with Content-Specific Vocabulary

- Don't overwhelm students with new vocabulary. Choose five to seven words that are vital for comprehension of the concept. Create **word walls** with the words and their meanings, prefixes, suffixes, and root words that are common to your subject area.

- Be aware of words with multiple meanings. A science teacher may use the word *grounding* while teaching a unit on electricity. When asked, a student may confidently nod that he knows the meaning—a punishment given to teenagers by their parents!

- Have students evaluate their understanding of key words using the KAU activity:

    1. *On the board or overhead, write a list of five to seven key words students will encounter in the text.*

    2. *Have each student draw three columns on his or her paper, labeling them with a plus sign, a check mark, and a minus sign.*

    3. *Students then categorize each of the words in this manner: if the student knows the word (K), it will be listed under the plus; if the student is aware of the word (A), but isn't sure of its meaning, it should be written in the check column; and if the word is unknown to the student (U), it will be listed under the minus sign.*

    4. *Students can then discuss the words in small groups or as a class prior to reading the text.*

62

Activating Prior Knowledge

- Use an anticipation/reaction guide: create a worksheet with six to eight statements regarding the concept to be taught. Prior to reading, have students label each statement with a T for true, F for false, or ? for "don't know." As students read, have them look for facts that will either support or alter their opinions about each statement. After reading, students should again label each statement with a T, F, or ?.

- Directed Reading/Thinking Activity: Prior to reading, students answer the following questions—*What I Know, What I Think I Know,* and *What I'll Learn.* After reading, *What I Know I Learned* is answered.

Adapting Texts for Struggling Readers

- With a few of your textbooks, use a highlighter pen to identify key concepts in a passage. Give these books to struggling readers to help them focus on what is most important in the reading.

- Give students partially filled-out graphic organizers with a list of words to be used in the blanks at the bottom of the page. As they read the text, students fill in the blanks to create the organizer.

- Have students use sticky-notes to mark sections of the text they do not understand.

adapted from: Classroom Connections:
Linking National Middle School Association
to middle level classrooms around the world.
Patti Kinney and Mary Beth Munroe. NMSA. 2003

- Another very helpful resource for reading strategies comes in the form of an article in Educational Leadership. In "Seven Literacy Strategies That Work," Fisher, Frey, and Williams (Nov. 2002) provide easy methods for content area teachers to implement in their classrooms.

Seven Literacy Strategies That Work

1. Read-Alouds

A read-aloud, or shared reading, is one of the most effective ways for young adults to hear fluent reading. (Allen, 2000)

For More Information on Read-Alouds:

Supporting Struggling Readers and Writers. Strickland, Ganske, and Monroe. pp. 123–125

Teaching Reading in Middle Schools. Orb. Chapter 8

Modifying the Four Blocks for Upper Grades: Matching Strategies to Students' Needs. Sigmon. p. 17

2. KWL Charts

KWL charts (Ogle, 1986) are a great way to hook students into learning. These language charts start with the question, "What do you *know* about the topic?" Following this discussion, students are asked, "What do you still *want to know* about the topic?" Once the unit of study has been completed, the language charts are used again and students answer the third question, "What did you *learn* about the topic?"

For More Information on KWL Charts:

Guided Comprehension. McLaughlin & Allen, 2002. pp. 119, 145, 146

Words, Words, Words. Allen. Chapter 2

Strategies for Integrating Reading and Writing. Harmon and Wood. pp. 51–53

Strategic Reading. Wilhelm, Baker, and Dube. pp. 114–116

50 Graphic Organizers. Bromly, DeVitis, and Modlo. pp. 48–49

When Kids Can't Read. Beers. pp. 80–87

3. Graphic Organizers

Graphic Organizers provide students with visual information that complements the class discussion or text. Organizers come in many forms (see Wood, Lapp, and Flood, 1992)

For More Information on Graphic Organizers:

Guided Comprehension. pp. 124, 142–164 (black line masters)

Dinah Zike. *Foldables* videotape

Supporting Struggling Readers and Writers. pp. 150, 152, 164

50 Graphic Organizers for Reading, Writing and More. Bromly, DeVitis, and Modlo.

4. Vocabulary Instruction

Focus on *transportable* vocabulary skills, i.e., skills that students can use across content areas (e.g., word families, prefixes, suffixes, word roots, vocabulary journals, and word walls). (See Blachowicz & Fisher, 2002.)

For More Information on Vocabulary Instruction:

Supporting Struggling Readers and Writers. pp. 109–113

Guided Comprehension. pp. 11–12, 44–46, 130

Words, Words, Words. Allen. Chapter 4

Modifying the Four Blocks for the Upper Grades. Sigmon. Chapter 6

When Kids Can't Read. Beers. Chapter 9

5. Writing to Learn

Reading, writing, and content learning are related. Teachers use writing-to-learn strategies at the beginning, middle, or end of class to help students inquire, clarify, or reflect upon the content. Writing helps students think about the content, reflect upon their knowledge of content, and share their thoughts with the teacher.

For More Information on Writing to Learn:

Reading Strategies That Work. Robb.1992. pp. 51–65

50 Graphic Organizers. Bromly, DeVitis, and Modlo. Part III

Modifying the Four Blocks for Upper Grades. Sigmon. Chapter 5

6. Structured Note-Taking

Students draw a vertical line about 2 inches from the left side of the paper, log main ideas and key words to the left and details to the right of the line, and write a brief summary of the lesson at the bottom of the page. This strategy leads to deeper student engagement and reflection (see Spires and Stone, 1989).

For More Information on Structured Note-Taking:

Guided Comprehension. pp. 122, 148–149

Supporting Struggling Readers and Writers. p. 203

A Handbook for Classroom Instruction That Works. Marzano, Norford, Paynter, Pickering and Gaddy. Module 6

7. Reciprocal Teaching

Reciprocal teaching allows students to become the instructors of the content that they are studying. Working in groups of four, the students read a text passage together, following a protocol for predicting, questioning, clarifying, and summarizing—skills that teachers have modeled over a series of lessons until students are comfortable assuming these assigned roles.

For More Information on Reciprocal Teaching:

Guided Comprehension. pp. 28–30, 140, 52–53

Prepare Your Professional Library

All teachers owe it to themselves and to their students to remain current in their professional reading. Would you want to be attended by a physician who had not read a professional journal or professional literature since graduating from medical school? Is teaching middle school so different? I don't think so.

The big difference is that doctors, perhaps, have more income with which they might make purchases of books and periodicals. If we have only a limited amount of disposable income with which to work, there are several books and periodicals that are "must haves" for the middle level practitioner. Among these are:

> **This We Believe: Successful Schools for Young Adolescents.** NMSA 2003

This We Believe is the National Middle School Association's position paper, which is a living document that is a clear, readable reflection of the middle school philosophy and understanding of the young adolescent and the conditions that make effective, developmentally appropriate middle schools. *This We Believe* is the bible for the middle level educator.

> **Turning Points 2000: Educating Adolescents in the 21st Century. A Report of the Carnegie Corporation of New York.** Anthony W. Jackson and Gayle A. Davis. Simultaneously published by NMSA and Teachers College Press. 2000

Turning Points 2000 is a revision of the earlier *Turning Points* of 1989. The updated version integrates what is known from education research and practice within a coherent approach toward adolescent education. This is a volume that educators can use in their own efforts to transform middle schools.

> **Teaching at the Middle Level: A Professional's Handbook.** Sandra L. Schurr, Julia Thomason, and Max Thompson. Edited by John H. Lounsbury. D. C. Heath and Company, 1996.

Although this book is several years old, it is a classic. In

Teaching at the Middle Level, teachers will find practically everything they ever wanted to know about teaching middle school, but were afraid to ask. Broken into six modules, this volume is a definite "must have!" The table of contents has to be viewed to understand the scope of the work:

Module 1: The Developmental Characteristics of Young Adolescents
Topics: Cognitive Development, Emotional Development, Physical Development, Social Development, and Character Development

Module 2: Making the Transition to the Middle School
Topics: Young Adolescents: A Refresher, Turning Points and Recommendations, the Transition Process, Philosophy and Mission Statements, Leadership Roles and Responsibilities, Teacher Roles and Responsibilities

Module 3: Middle School Program Components
Topics: General Components and Characteristics, Teaming in the Middle School, The Advisory Program in the Middle School, Expanded Exploratories, Electives and Intramurals, Flexible Block Scheduling, Flexible Student Grouping

Module 4: Middle School Curriculum
Topics: Curriculum Frameworks, Learning Unite, Thinking Skills Curriculum, Whole Language in the Middle School, Outcome-Based Curriculum

Module 5: Middle School Instructional Strategies
Topics: The Lecture Method, The Case Study Method, Games and Simulations, Role Playing, Cooperative Learning, Creative Thinking, Critical Thinking, Investigation Task Cards, Multiple Intelligences, Interdisciplinary Instruction, Contracts and Learning Activity Packets, Graphic Organizers for Thinking,

Reports, Instructional Technology, Teaching in the Culturally Diverse Middle School Classroom, English as a Second Language

Module 6: Assessment
Topics: Authentic Assessment, Product Assessment, Portfolio Assessment, Performance Assessment, Response Journals and Learning Logs, Observations and Interviews, Self-Assessment Tools and Techniques, Norm-Referenced and Criterion-Referenced Tests, Grades and Grading

Day One & Beyond: Practical Matters for New Middle-Level Teachers.
Rick Wormeli. Simultaneously published by NMSA and Stenhouse Publishers. 2003.

Based on his many years of research and experience in the middle level classroom, Rick Wormeli offers front-line advice on: practical survival matters, such as what to do the first day and week, setting up the grade book and other record keeping, and what to do if you only have one computer in the classroom; classroom management, including discipline, getting students' attention, and roving classrooms; social issues, like the unique nature of middle level students, relating to students, and positive relations with parents; professional concerns, from collegiality with teammates to professional resources all middle level teachers should have.

not much, just chillin': the hidden lives of middle schoolers.
Linda Perlstein. Farrar, Straus and Giroux, New York. 2003.

". . . *not much, just chillin* . . . takes the reader to a mysterious place—the changing world of the middle schooler—never before visited in this personal way. Every parent, teacher, principal, and friend of an adolescent can gain useful insights from this book. Linda Perlstein has done a great service for education by spending a year with these boys and girls in their classrooms and homes, and then eloquently chronicling their complicated lives."
—Richard Riley, former Secretary of Education

Web Resources for First-Year Middle Level Teachers

The Internet is not a substitute for a wise, caring mentor or a break in the day to plan a new lesson. But going online can do a lot to reduce some of the isolation that new teachers face. In particular, the Internet offers research, tips, lesson plans, discussion groups, and a treasure trove of data that can be easily downloaded. The following resources, most of which are free, are a sampling of what is available:

http://NMSA.org

The National Middle School Association home page. Wonderful resources designed especially for the middle level professional.

http://kmsaonline.com

Home page to the Kentucky Middle School Association. Information and links to current opportunities at the middle level.

http://middleweb.com

Designed especially for the middle level, Middle Web provides one-stop shopping for any who visit. Discussion groups are especially useful.

www.teachnet.org

Teach net: lesson plans, online discussions, ideas exchange, articles, and research.

www.enc.org/

Eisenhower National Clearing House for Mathematics and Science Education: reform ideas, lessons, software, professional development opportunities, and links to online academic standards.

www.ed.gov.free/

Federal Resources for Educational Excellence: online learning resources available from the U. S. government agencies.

Prepare and Update Your Portfolio

You may have been required to keep a portfolio as a student teacher or intern, but it is wise to *choose* to update your portfolio on an ongoing basis. Your portfolio captures the highlights of your career. Strut your stuff! Document your successes. Keep documentation to establish your credentials when applying for other positions in education at a later date. Add materials to your portfolio that chart your progress this first year and throughout your career. Among other things, include:

- Your educational philosophy
- Your teaching certificate and updated individual professional growth plan
- Transcripts of degrees and postgraduate work
- Evaluations, awards, honors
- Professional organization affiliations
- Sample lesson plans with corresponding photos or samples of student work
- A videotape of a presentation or activity you have facilitated
- Samples of individual student work showing growth over time
- Flyers from conferences you attend

Prepare to be Reflective

Becoming lifelong learners is a great part of teaching at the middle level. Because we care so deeply for the young adolescents we teach, we continually try to create a developmentally responsive classroom environment for them. But, we must remember to nurture our own growth simultaneously.

Developing the habit of mind of reflecting on our teaching practice is of crucial importance. Spend time regularly reflecting on your positive and negative experiences, your successes and failures. Continually refine your teaching. Now and then, take time to self-assess. The following checklist may be helpful.

On the Road to Lifelong Learning

☐ Am I self-disciplined? Am I well prepared for class, on time, and organized? Even if I am having a bad day, do I show students proper respect?

☐ Do I clarify my expectations? Do I set clear limits and consequences for behavior? Do my students have learning goals?

☐ Do I enforce rules with fairness for all students?

☐ Do I help students feel secure and free from threat in my classroom?

☐ Do I greet students and ask about their interests? Do I have individual conferences with students who are having problems in my class?

☐ Do I emphasize cooperation over competition?

☐ Do I use a variety of teaching strategies and tell students how a topic or skill they are learning is useful or relevant to their lives?

☐ Do I maintain a brisk instructional pace and make smooth transitions between activities?

☐ Do I give students immediate constructive feedback? Do I deal with misbehavior as quickly as possible?

☐ Do I recognize the success, improvements, and contributions of individual students?

☐ Do I teach students self-monitoring skills?

☐ Do I enlist parents' help and show them how to contribute to their children's education?

adapted from: *First-Class Teacher*. Canter and Associates.1998.

Reflective Questions About a Lesson

Becoming a reflective teacher requires time and practice. Below are sample questions you may use to practice reflective writing.

Think About the Lesson.

- What lesson did you teach?
- Why have you selected this lesson?

Describe the Lesson.

- To which class/group did you teach this lesson?
- What are the demographics of this group (race, gender, age, etc.)?
- What was the content of the lesson?
- When did you teach the lesson (time of day)?
- Where does the lesson fit in your curriculum? Unit plan?
- What did you teach before this lesson? After?
- What were your expected outcomes?
- What did you and your students do during the lesson/roles you all played?
- What kinds of questions did you ask?

Analyze Your Teaching of the Lesson.

- How did you present the material?
- How are students engaged in learning?
- Did students react to one another as well as to you?
- How did things go? What was your overall feeling?
- How did you measure what students learned?
- Did you relate this to previous learning or students' shared experiences?
- How did you account for diversity in the lesson?

What Worked and Didn't Work?

- What was effective/ineffective about your teaching techniques in this lesson?
- Did you achieve desired outcomes?
- Were there outcomes achieved that you did not expect or plan for?
- How did students react to the materials you chose or the methods you used?
- Did the lesson achieve or help achieve a class or school goal?
- How does this lesson relate to your philosophy of education?
- Describe the environment. Did it allow for intellectual comfort/risk-taking?

What Are Your Next Steps?

- What techniques/materials from this lesson will you continue to use?
- Which ones will you stop using or modify? Why?
- Based on how well the students learned the material, what will you do next?
- How will you continue to develop your personal teaching techniques based on the internal/external feedback from this lesson?
- What did you learn from your students?

Prepare to be Successful

Good Teaching: The Top Ten Requirements

By Richard Leblanc, York University, Ontario

1. Good teaching is as much about passion as it is about reason. It's about not only motivating students to learn,

but teaching them how to learn, and doing so in a manner that is relevant, meaningful, and memorable. It's about caring for your craft, having a passion for it, and conveying that passion to everyone, most importantly to your students.

2. Good teaching is about substance and treating students as consumers of knowledge. It's about doing your best to keep on top of your field, reading sources, inside and outside of your areas of expertise, and being at the leading edge as often as possible. But knowledge is not confined to scholarly journals. Good teaching is also about bridging the gap between theory and practice. It's about leaving the ivory tower and immersing oneself in the field, talking to, consulting with, and assisting practitioners, and liaising with their communities.

3. Good teaching is about listening, questioning, being responsive, and remembering that each student and class is different. It's about eliciting responses and developing the oral communication skills of the quiet students. It's about pushing students to excel; at the same time, it's about being human, respecting others, and being professional at all times.

4. Good teaching is about not always having a fixed agenda and being rigid, but being flexible, fluid, experimenting, and having the confidence to react and adjust to changing circumstances. It's about getting only 10 percent of what you wanted to do in a class done, and still feeling good. It's about deviating from the course syllabus or lecture schedule easily when there is more and better learning elsewhere. Good teaching is about the creative balance between being an authoritarian dictator on the one hand and a pushover on the other.

5. Good teaching is also about style. Should good teaching be entertaining? You bet! Does this mean that it lacks in substance? Not a chance! Effective teaching is not about being locked with both hands glued to a podium or having your eyes fixed on a slide projector while you drone on.

Good teachers work the room and every student in it. They realize that they are the conductors and the class is the orchestra. All students play different instruments, and at varying proficiencies.

6. This is very important—good teaching is about humor. It's about being self-deprecating and not taking yourself too seriously. It's often about making innocuous jokes, mostly at your own expense, so that the ice breaks and students learn in a more relaxed atmosphere where you, like them, are human with your own share of faults and shortcomings.

7. Good teaching is about caring, nurturing, and developing minds and talents. It's about devoting time, often invisible, to every student. It's also about the thankless hours of grading, designing or redesigning courses, and preparing materials to still further enhance instruction.

8. Good teaching is supported by strong and visionary leadership, and very tangible institutional support— resources, personnel, and funds. Good teaching is continually reinforced by an overarching vision that transcends the entire organization and is reflected in what is said, but more importantly by what is done.

9. Good teaching is about mentoring between senior and junior faculty, teamwork, and being recognized and promoted by one's peers. Effective teaching should also be rewarded, and poor teaching needs to be remedied through training and development programs.

10. At the end of the day, good teaching is about having fun, experiencing pleasure and intrinsic rewards . . . like locking eyes with a student in the back row and seeing the synapses and neurons connecting, thoughts being formed, the person becoming better, and a smile cracking across a face as learning all of a sudden happens. Good teachers practice their craft not for the money or because they have to, but because they truly enjoy it and because they want to. Good teachers couldn't imagine doing anything else.

PART 5

Keys to Success
for New Teachers

To Catch Them When They Fall

They come to you with fears
They come to you with dreams
They come to you and share their secret hopes
Some come with broken histories
Some come from perfect families
Some come with scars that they may never show
But still they're here
Standing in front of you
Still they're here

CHORUS: You try to teach them how to fly
You want to see them soar
Keep your eyes upon the sky
You wish you could do more
But there's only one of you
And you can't save them all
Sometimes the best that you can do
Is to catch them when they fall

Sometimes you just want silence
Sometimes you need some peace
Sometimes you need to lay those burdens down
Sometimes there's so much laughter
You think you'll never cry
Sometimes it's the other way around
Still they're here, standing in front of you
Still they're here

CHORUS

CHORUS

To Catch Them When They Fall
Written by: Monte Selby / Mark Selby / Tia Sillers ©℗Street Singer Music, BMI /
Blue Otis Music /Songs of Moraine, BMI / Choice Is Tragic Music /Ensign Music Corporation, BMI
Produced by: Mark Selby & Monte Selby. Executive Producer Mark Meckel

Be Reasonable

- You probably went into education because you care about kids and you want to make a difference in their lives. However, be reasonable. *You will not save them all.* You'll be doing well your first year if you can just stay positive and have lessons ready every hour of every day. You will not be able to make every student leave your class feeling like that was the most worthwhile class he will have all day.

- Don't expect lots of positive feedback from students. *Students complain* no matter what effort you put into your lessons. Just be sure to have an educational objective/reason to back up everything you do in class. And don't expect students to jump for joy at your efforts to make class more interesting. Be patient, they may come back next year when they are no longer your students and reminisce about the good times they had in your classroom.

- You have many great ideas for your classroom that you'd like to be able to do. *But you can't do it all your first year.* Or any year, for that matter. There are always better ways of doing what you're doing. Don't let that frustrate you.

- Teaching is an art, not a science. It will take time for you to find a comfortable teaching style, and it will change a little every year. Methods that work for some will not work for others. There is no "right" way to teach. You must *find the way that works for you*.

Organize Your Life

- Although this sounds harsh, *don't expect to have much of a life* outside of student teaching or your first year of teaching. Beginning teachers need almost every waking moment to be prepared for the classroom. Say good-bye to television for a while, say good-bye to late-night chats with friends. You need to prepare and you need sleep. That is all you have time for!

Getting Off on the Right Foot: Part 5

- But, by the same token, *Try not to let your new teacher habits make their way into your home and marriage!* If your husband does something annoying, don't give him the teacher's "evil eye." You will soon know the one I am referring to! Don't interrupt a perfectly good argument to say things like, "Let's think about our choices!" When you are at home, give it up! Don't scold, don't correct, and don't try to be the model of perfection. Yes, many people do expect teachers to know everything and do everything perfectly, but don't fall for that trap. When you leave school for the day, just become Mama, or Daddy, Hubby, or Better Half! And, for goodness sake, *take time for yourself!* Watch something totally stupid and pointless on TV, listen to "un-teachery" music, call an old friend (and don't talk about school). Try not to feel guilty for taking time for yourself and your family occasionally. A little time invested in purely selfish, joyful activities can go a long way toward making you a better, more positive person in the classroom.

- *Strive for balance in your life!* Look beyond the petty annoyances and hassles, both big and small, and try to remember why you became a teacher in the first place. Maybe you became a teacher so you could make a difference in the lives of children or to share yourself with the world! Keep your reasons for teaching close to your heart and you'll soon realize that all of the stress really can be worth it.

- Do as much ahead of time as you can to get ready for school. *Find a lesson plan format* you can use. Find a method of keeping grades that will help you keep your sanity. (I have to turn in grades for athletic and other extracurricular eligibility every single week.) That is what computers are for!

- After you complete a unit, take a few minutes to jot down some impressions about how the unit worked. *List changes* that you should make before teaching it again. This will save you the heartache of making the same mistakes twice, and it makes the second year easier.

- *It is okay if you are only a day or two ahead in your lessons.* Many veteran teachers will be at least a week ahead, and will have good ideas of what they will be teaching next month. Don't worry, I've never met a new teacher who was able to do this. Have assurance that you are not alone in the desperate grasp for ideas for a unit you start in two days.

Organize Your Time

As you consider how you use the limited amount of time available each day, it is necessary to prioritize task vs. time needs. Perhaps it will help to ask yourself several questions each morning, and jot down your answers for your own reference. Develop a form such as the one on page 95.

Guiding Questions:

1. What are the three most important things I need to accomplish today?

2. How can I best accomplish these tasks? What should I delegate to others?

3. How would it affect my day if I did not accomplish these tasks?

Three Top Tasks:

1. _____
2. _____
3. _____

How will I accomplish them?

What can I delegate?

What will I do *only* if I have enough time?

Reflect

- Although the first years of teaching seem to consume you, you do need to stop to reflect on how you are doing. *Make short notes* about how policies work, how units went, and think about how you treat your students. After all, we are there for the students, and there is more than content to teaching. However, this is difficult to see the first year.

- *Take compliments seriously and criticism lightly.* I feel like I make more mistakes than I do good. But we can't let this get us down. Mistakes are how we learn. Take the compliments you get and put them in a "warm fuzzy" file to pull out on a rainy day.

- *Share, share, and share!* You must have someone to confide in. A spouse or significant other is fine, but it really ought to be someone in the teaching field—a mentor teacher, or even a new or student teacher. Many times just talking about frustrations and joys gives you insight about the situation that you hadn't seen before.

- *Share materials.* Most teachers take it as a compliment that you want to copy their units. It is much easier having something to work from, something to build on, something you can change to fit your teaching style.

- *Write out your philosophy* and have it handy. On days you wonder why you went into the profession of education, pull it out, and remember your reasons for becoming a teacher.

- *Have ways of encouraging yourself.* Maybe it is a favorite poem, story, or audio/video tape. Mine is an audio tape of Guy Dud that came from one of Dr. James Dobson's *Focus on the Family* radio shows. Guy Dud was Teacher of the Year, 1986–1987. He entertains, encourages, and reminds me that I am in the right profession.

- *Take time for non-education reflection.* You need to remain sane for your sake—and for your students' sake. Many times it will be difficult to do this, but I found that when I was stressed the most, I wasn't giving myself time to be "off-duty." Enjoy music, quiet time, and moments just to be thankful for what you have.

Prepare to Listen to the Voice of Experience!

50 More Crucial Tips for New Teachers

1 Be nice to the secretaries, avoid the bus drivers, and don't let your room get too messy. Those staff members are often the informal CIA and FBI. Your reputation may depend largely on what these people report informally to their supervisors and the public.

2 Never apologize in class about the curriculum. Don't ever tell students your lesson might not be as good as planned, or that you forgot to bring the tape recorder, or that the ditto should have been clearer, or that you forgot their papers, or whatever you want to apologize for. Students are critical enough already without your adding fuel to their fires and giving them the unintended message you admit you are incompetent. Besides, some students undoubtedly thought everything was fine and no one knew what they were missing, so leave apologies for personal matters.

3 When you are leading a class discussion and a student asks a question softly—be sure to repeat the question so everyone hears it. Tend to move away from a student you are addressing (while maintaining good eye contact), so that the student speaks more loudly and thus can be heard by everyone. Also, often when you've asked a question simultaneously answered by multiple students, you will inadvertently hear only the correct answer. However, all the students may not know which of the many they heard was correct. Tend to repeat a correct student answer.

4 By the end of the first day, know every student's name. This helps rapport and discipline.

5 Minimize extra directions or repeating directions to the entire class. Circulate to see that your directions were understood properly.

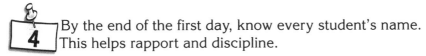

6 Running a class is like an airplane trip. The danger usually lies in the "takeoff" and in the landing. Monitor the ingress and egress of your class to avoid problems and to create a positive learning environment.

7 Don't ask poor questions such as, "How many have read . . . " It tends to inculcate dishonesty.

8 Theodore Roethke contends "the cardinal sin of an educator is to be boring." Make your class interesting; make the quality of life in your class agreeable.

9 A well-taught class mitigates against discipline problems.

10 Variety is the spice of curriculum as well as life. Vary your teaching strategies.

11 You don't have to cover in class everything you expect students to learn. That's what texts and homework are for.

12 A meaningful activity-based curriculum works. From John Dewey to Leslie Hart educators have verified we learn by doing.

13 Circulate. When you circulate through your class you help keep students on task; help clarify and instruct students who need help; have opportunity for friendly, personal interaction with others. And you can give special help to those behind and slow down those ahead so the class finishes about the same time.

14 Put assignments on the board. And when students ask what they are supposed to do—just point at the board. It saves time and energy.

15 No permanent potty pass! Especially no tire irons or hub caps or other passes that will never be lost. If a kid has to go, be interrupted. It discourages unwarranted use of the request. If a kid needs to go a lot, the student has a bladder problem or you need to talk to the student about how to make the course more enjoyable or at least more possible. Another idea is to have a non-publicized three potty pass limit that you tell the student privately about after two trips. If the student needs to go a fourth time, okay it, but require an after class or after school discussion to stay honest with the intent of the policy.

16 If you can get the class involved in a self-directed activity, you can spend time with individuals or small groups who need special help.

17 If materials are required for class, meet students at the door to remind them prior to the start of class.

18 Step outside your subject to solve whatever problems are in your way. If your class members aren't listening to each other, do a communications lesson regardless of your subject matter. If your talented chorus doesn't look like a group of winners, teach poise.

19 Scan the class at unpredictable times, especially during tests. A favorite trick of mine is to identify someone doing something he shouldn't, like chewing gum, and then while my back is turned, ask him to throw it away. Cultivate the misconception that you have eyes in the back of your head.

20 Don't leave your keys out EVER!
EVER!

21 Tolerate ambiguity. Don't try to make everything black and white. Emerson says a "foolish consistency is the hobgoblin of little minds." Leave yourself room for adjustments.

22 Teach to your test. Your test should measure your objectives, so you should be teaching the skills you measure.

23 Teach your students how to study, read, and write for your particular subject area. Don't assume the English teacher (or anyone else) can do that for you.

24 Show an interest in students' extracurricular activities. Ask about the teams, the clubs, the dances, the awards.

25 Make your learning environment attractive. Display student work. Highlight your subject matter with displays and posters. Students are very likely to retain this material they look at while otherwise not paying attention.

26 Make 'em go home reciting Shakespeare. He's good P.R. and every student knows it's not only part of our cultural heritage, but also what every "good" school makes its students learn. Do, however, pick a good passage that's not too long.

27 Keep them guessing. Be a bit off the wall. Occasionally do something unexpected. When you are not totally predictable, it keeps them alert, less likely to mess with you, and interested.

28 Appreciate differences. You've spent all your years finding out who you are and what you like and dislike. But now, as the teacher, you need to appreciate all the tastes, foods, human values, cultural backgrounds of all your students. If you strive toward diversity in your instruction, you can give every student a chance to succeed at something and to improve at something else.

29 Allow no one to go into your desk. It compromises your authority. That's your private area.

30 Laugh if it's funny. Don't be threatened.

31 Teach to your strengths.

32 Don't make everything competitive.

33 Be flexible. Don't paint yourself into a corner with arbitrary rules.

34 Ask students when they want tests. That way you can avoid scheduling a test on the day of the physics quiz or on the day after the Super Bowl. You'll be seen as a decent human being. And you'll get better results and fewer complaints about scores.

35 If your class is getting unruly or a little out of hand, give them a quiet seat assignment and call them one by one to come sit at your desk while you show them in "The Record Book" their string of grades for the term. This puts the troublesome students on notice; makes them a little wary; sobers them a bit; helps get them back on task. You, in the meantime, can enjoy their discomfort while being very encouraging about how you know they are smart and can still do okay in your class. It is amazing how mesmerized some students become by a grade book.

36 Divide and conquer. I like to divide my class up into four sections with a lane down the middle going from side to side of the classroom. I prefer my desk in the rear of one of the sections. If I absolutely have to talk to the entire class I go to the middle where the two lanes cross and I can be the center of attention. Otherwise the four sections are convenient for small group or seat work. If I'm having trouble with a small group, I can isolate the group without distracting the other groups. Divide and conquer. If I'm having trouble with an individual student, I try to get him or her outside for a personal discussion. Divide and conquer.

37 CYA. Cover your assets. It's helpful to know which onsite administrator you can best trust. If you hear a rumor that involves you—for example, a student in your class was "seen" under the influence of alcohol—there's a good chance others have also heard the rumor. I think it is wise to informally inform the trusted administrator something like, "I've heard a rumor so-and-so was under the influence of alcohol in my class, but I couldn't tell it. I'll continue to watch for a problem." This communicates that you

88

are on top of things, and should the administration pick this rumor up elsewhere, you've helped them cover their assets.

38 If you absolutely need administrative help, use it. But administrators are exceedingly busy people, too, and they want to feel that you are basically a competent person before they help you with an unusual problem. Administrators often become defensive when you bring up a problem, because it usually means it will be time consuming for them and probably impossible to solve anyway. So mention a problem (that unbeknownst to them you have already solved very successfully), watch them tense up defensively, and then share how you solved the problem. In their relief they will be most congratulatory and supportive, you will have won points, and they will be less defensive and more helpful should you later have a problem you really can't solve.

39 If you are going to require that students be seated at the end-of-class bell, make them go back to their seats before the bell rings to dismiss them, not after the bell has already rung. If the bell has already rung, not only might you look foolish when you are unable to control their exit, but you also might be trampled to death.

40 Try not to get mad at kids and blame them when they aren't doing what they are supposed to, when down deep inside you know it's because you are ill prepared, or previously upset, or haven't thought through your assignment.

41 All of your assignments do not have to be evaluated for a letter grade. Some can be "criterion referenced." If they meet the basic criterion, the student receives full credit. Excellence is its own reward. This allays a lot of fears and nit-picking about differences in grades on tasks with unclear criteria for success.

42 Now that your lesson is exceedingly well-conceived and prepared, you've still got to sell it to your class. This will "be really fun," or "interesting," or "helpful in college," or will "keep you from flunking." It is much easier to sell something you do believe in, but you still need to sell it.

43 Just as I think you should teach to your test (because it measures what you wanted students to learn), I think you should teach to your "Course Evaluations." If it is important to "organize" your subject matter, point out how your subject matter is organized. If you want students to enjoy "music," point out the times they are enjoying music. Help students make the connections between the purposes and the results. Then ask students how well your particular class made those connections.

44 The overwhelming advantage of a cumulative final is that you can hold out to your worst student the prospect of still passing (if only barely so) your course. Any other decision on your part invites a discipline nightmare from the moment the student realizes she or he cannot pass your class until the last minute of that class.

45 Pay attention to the extracurricular events on campus and compliment students in your classes for work well done.

46 THE ONLY WAY TO HAVE A HAPPY AND WORTHWHILE TEACHING CAREER IS TO TEACH STUDENTS, NOT JUST SUBJECT MATTER. With all the time I have spent in school I hope I do not have to explain that I think subject matter is incredibly important. But if you are letting any particular subject stand between you and your students, you won't have any fun, you'll be frustrated all the time, and teaching will get worse each year instead of better. Get on the students' side; you can still give the A's to those who do best on the subject; but you can truly like all your students regardless of how much they like what you are teaching.

47 Since "being controlled" is equated with "being cared for," attempts are frequently made to test the severity or strictness of superordinate authority to see if it remains firm. If intended (or executed) rebellion produces swift and firm sanctions, the individual is reassured, at the same time that he is complaining bitterly at the injustice of being caught and punished.

48 The guilt squeeze tends to work with middle class kids, and specific sanctions/punishments with working class kids. But as with all generalizations, they aren't much help in figuring out your 30 to 40 students per class. From my experience you cannot predict which kids respond to which kind of discipline except through trial and error. But as a beginning teacher I found it hard to be tough in the face of vociferous complaints until I realized a lot of kids equate such toughness/fairness with caring.

49 Games (Some) Faculty Play. Although teachers' lots are generally better than they have been for the last 4,000 years, working conditions have deteriorated for the first time in history over the past 10 to 20 years (salary, class size, seriousness of student problems). But even before the slippage there is something about teaching that has attracted many chronic complainers. They especially enjoy sharing their complaints with new teachers, and do so ad infinitum. I have found only one way to make this interaction tolerable—I play a game I call "It's Really a Lot Worse than You Realize." It is a variation of a routine Monty Python has where the tuxedoed discussants argue on who really had it worse growing up and the "winner" lived under the hole in the road. No matter how bleak a picture your chronically complaining fellow teacher paints, with a little imagination and real or imagined data you can explain why.

50 Since wizened and grizzled veteran teachers will invariably think you, as a beginning teacher, will be too easy on kids I highly recommend that you give them the respect that is their due and periodically seek their advice publicly, ordinarily in the faculty lounge, on whether, indeed, you are grading too hard, giving too many assignments, and lecturing too much, regardless of what you actually happen to be doing. This goes over much better than your explanations of how well your "new" ideas are working in your classroom.

From http://arachnid.pepperdine.edu/goseweb/teachertips.htm

Prepare to Laugh

You Know You Really Teach Middle School If . . .

. . . you empty your pockets at night and find
    1. two used hall passes
    2. one unused bus pass
    3. a pencil stub
    4. no money (you spent your change in the faculty room candy stash)
    5. a note with a drawing of Satan and two expletives that needed deleting

. . . you brag to your spouse about how many parent phone calls you got done today

. . . your relatives refuse to attend one of your parties if "it's going to be mostly teachers" because they all talk shop

. . . you walk the halls of your building and unconsciously pick up litter

. . . you are irritated by adults who chew gum in public

. . . your spouse surreptitiously reads the paper at dinner while you describe your day

. . . you plan your seating chart so that the short kids can't hide behind bigger ones

. . . you have seen firsthand what gum wrappers and pennies can do to a floppy disk drive

. . . you write your name conspicuously on all personal objects, including your car keys, your masking tape, your textbook, and your chair

. . . you sometimes choose to pretend not to hear comments that were perfectly intelligible to everyone else who was in the room

. . . you know what your classroom door sounds like when slammed mightily

. . . you have classroom rules about where people may put their feet

. . . you tell subtle jokes just to see those few smiles of the ones that catch on

. . . your class gladly acknowledges that they watch Letterman and Rosie O'Donnell and MTV, but tell you they haven't time to look at something by PBS during prime time

. . . you despise Halloween candy, Christmas candy, and Valentine candy

. . . your students prefer current events stories that deal with rape, murder, electrocution, and demonic possession

. . . one of your students writes to Congress (on your nickel) to complain about some cigarette butts thrown into a local lake

. . . you still can't believe you allowed yourself to be sucked into an argument regarding whether Beanie Babies should be allowed in class

. . . you know at least three ways to remove objectionable doodles from textbooks so the next user will not be offended

. . . your team goes out for dinner to celebrate the news that your biggest headache is moving to another district

. . . you clean desks yourself just to keep the place looking nice and to help your own morale

. . . a mother calls to chew you out because you have ignored her son's project only to learn from you that it must be the one that has sat on the chalk rail for weeks with the words, "Whose? Is this yours?" written above it

. . . your colleagues claim you inspected a blank student agenda in study hall and said, "Let me guess: All your teachers have been absent for the last month and a half."

from: www.teachingheart.net

Getting Off on the Right Foot: Part 5

Use with page 29.

Identify the Core Content to Be Learned:

Step 1. Review any prerequisite knowledge that will lead easily into the new curriculum.

_____

_____

_____

_____

Step 2. Core Content Lesson (what the teacher and students do). Be sure to include exact examples, problems, projects, or activities that will be used.

_____

_____

_____

_____

Step 3. Review and stress again all of the most important points of the core lesson.

_____

_____

_____

_____

Assess (evaluate) how well the new curriculum has been learned.

_____

_____

_____

_____

_____

_____

94

Use with page 35.

Student Data Sheet

Full name: _____

Name I wish to be called: _____

Address: _____

_____

Phone Number: _____

Name of parent(s) with whom you live: _____

_____

Number of brothers and sisters: _____

Any pets? What? Names? _____

_____

Complete the following statements:

If my home were a food, it would taste like . . . _____

_____

If my family were a noise, it would sound like . . . _____

_____

The animal I most resemble now is . . . _____

_____

If I could meet any person from history, it would be . . . _____

_____

My favorite subject is . . . _____

_____

My worst subject is . . . _____

_____

In order to teach me better, you should understand . . . _____

_____

_____

_____

Use with page 81.

Guiding Questions:

1. What are the three most important things I need to accomplish today?

2. How can I best accomplish these tasks? What should I delegate to others?

3. How would it affect my day if I did not accomplish these tasks?

Three Top Tasks:

1.

2.

3.

How will I accomplish them?

What can I delegate?

What will I do *only* if I have enough time?